Not Only Journals VIP Club

Join our VIP Club where we'll notify you anytime there is a special offer. Visit the link below, put your email in the box and you will be the first to know of our new releases, freebies, discounts and giveaways.

http://NotOnlyJournals.com/VIPaccess/

Made in United States
Orlando, FL
24 November 2021

10713813R00065